It's Always You Mommy

Written by
Dawn Sher-Rè Barclift

Illustrated by
Ros Webb

Copyright © 2018

All rights reserved.

No part of this book may be reproduced or transmitted in any form or by any means without the permission of the author. Any person who violates this copyright shall be pursued and prosecuted to the fullest extent of Local, State and Federal Law in accordance with the United States Constitution, so help me God.

Published by:

Dawn Barclift

THE CHILDREN'S BREAD

PUBLISHING HOUSE

Montclair, NJ 07042 childrensbreadd@gmail.com

Dedications To

God, the Father, Son and Holy Ghost for loving and covering me with Grace and Mercy in the midst of all my mess. For leading and guiding me into all truth, when man says differently. For the reality of knowing and understanding that "I can do all things" because you strengthen me.

My Gift of Love, Manny for being the wondrous and precious gift I gladly call "Son." I wouldn't change our journey for anything. I'd gladly answer the call and take on the position of being your "Single Mom" over and over again. I am proud of you. Loving you beyond forever, but God loves you more.

Mom, for always praying. For giving all of her children a foundation in Christ. For my first unselfish example of what it was to be a Single Mom, hocking wedding rings and more to take care of the "DARTS." Yet even more so, just for standing.

Dad, my first lesson of what a "good man" and father is. It's because of you that I have no doubt all men are NOT the same. Miss you always and forever.

My siblings: Lisa, Dorian, Natè, Damon, for making the job of a Single Mom doable, although you weren't obligated to do so. It's because of you + Mommy, that Manny knows love and has a strong and solid foundation. You are his village and he is your community property. I thank each of you for this.

Latisha, Gem, Pastor Carol, Yani, Paulette, Byron, and Gail, for praying, the encouragement, pep talks, for giving me an ear, for loving on and caring for Manny, for continually loving and believing in me, even when I wanted to stop. To all the **"Do Right" Single Mommies and Daddies** who found and find it not robbery to do right by their children. There's a blessing in the pressing.

Bong, bong, bong, bong, bong, bong, bong, bong, chimed the big hall clock. Justin was five years old. He did not yet know how to tell time except when he heard how many times the old grandfather clock rung. Eight times, the old clock rang. "Ooh, it's 8:00" Justin said with excitement.

Mommy opened the door to Justin's room. "Okay, I've given you your bath, so hmm… I'm wondering what comes next?" she asked playing a joke on him.

"Oh Mommy, you know what comes next. You can't fool me. It's our story time! But Mommy, tonight I don't want to read a story. I want to talk." "Okay" Mommy looked at Justin with a little bit of surprise. "Now what would you like to talk about baby?"

At that moment, Justin held his mommy's hand and feeling how warm it was; he laid his head on her shoulder. Although he was growing up, he liked laying his head on his mommy.

It made him feel like a little baby again.

"Mommy, when I wake up in the morning, you always have a hug for me. You make breakfast for me, so my tummy won't talk later. You wash and iron my clothes, shine my shoes and dress me. Mommy, you take me to school, even when I don't want to go."

"You taught me how to ride a bike, fish, fly an airplane and even throw a ball. When I fall and get a boo-boo, you make it better with hugs, kisses and a band-aid. I know you go to your job and do lots and lots of work so that I can have nice things."

"Then you come home, help me with my homework, give me supper, say prayers with me, kiss me goodnight and tuck me into bed."

"Oops!" Justin said as he remembered one more thing.

"You even find time to read me a bedtime story.

You must be a Super Mom!"

"It's always you Mommy… You're always there when I need you. But where is my daddy? Why isn't he with us? Sometimes I see some of the other kids at school with their daddies, and my daddy never comes to my school. Sometimes it makes me so sad inside."

"My classmates Lena and Wyatt's daddies don't come to school either. I wonder if it makes them sad too. Why is it always you Mommy, why?"

Mommy looked lovingly into Justin's big brown eyes; she put her arms around him and gave him a big hug and a kiss on the forehead. "Are you sad Mommy?" asked a very concerned Justin. Justin's mommy smiled a big smile. "Oh no honey, I'm not sad. I'm glad because my baby is really growing up."

"The first thing I want you to know is, your daddy does think about you." "But does my daddy love me?" Justin asked waiting to hear his mommy's answer. "Some people show their love differently" mommy explained. "Some people give hugs and kisses, some write love letters or make nice things like the pretty picture you made for me in school."

"Some people are afraid to show their love." Justin thought that was silly. "Afraid? Mommy, when I grow up, I will never be afraid to say I love you."

"I want you to understand; not all daddies are alike. Some daddies, like Lena's daddy or Wyatt's daddy, may not be around because they have to go to work far away, on a train or sometimes even a plane."

Some daddies aren't around because they had to go back to heaven to be with God.

There are some daddies who have even lost their way." "Is that what happened to my daddy? Did he lose his way?" Mommy gently smiled and answered, "Yes, your daddy lost his way."

Justin sat quietly for a moment and thought about what mommy had just said. "Are there other daddies who have lost their way too?" "Yes, baby. There are many other daddies that have lost their way too" Mommy answered.

Justin had an idea. "I know we can call 9-1-1 and ask the police to find him."

"Ha, ha, ha, ha, ha" mommy's laughter had the sound of love in her voice. "Oh my sweet Justin, it's not the kind of lost we need to call the police for."

"It's the kind of lost almost like Mommy driving around and around, not knowing which way to go, until I'm able to find my way back home again." "I sure hope daddy finds his way soon." Justin said with a little bit of hope in his voice.

"Well now honey, you have the most important job to do while daddy is trying to find his way" mommy explained. "With all your might, with all your heart and soul, you have to pray for daddy and wish him well wherever he is. And Mommy will too."

"I can do that job," Justin said proudly. "The most important thing you need to know," Mommy said, "Is that I love you so much. While I can't make daddy find his way, I'll be here to listen and give you all the love when you need it."

"Do you still miss daddy?" Justin asked curiously. "Sometimes. But I've got the best part of him in you" mommy answered as she began tickling him.

And through all the tickling and through all the laughter, Justin told her "I'm glad it's always you Mommy, I'm glad it's always you."

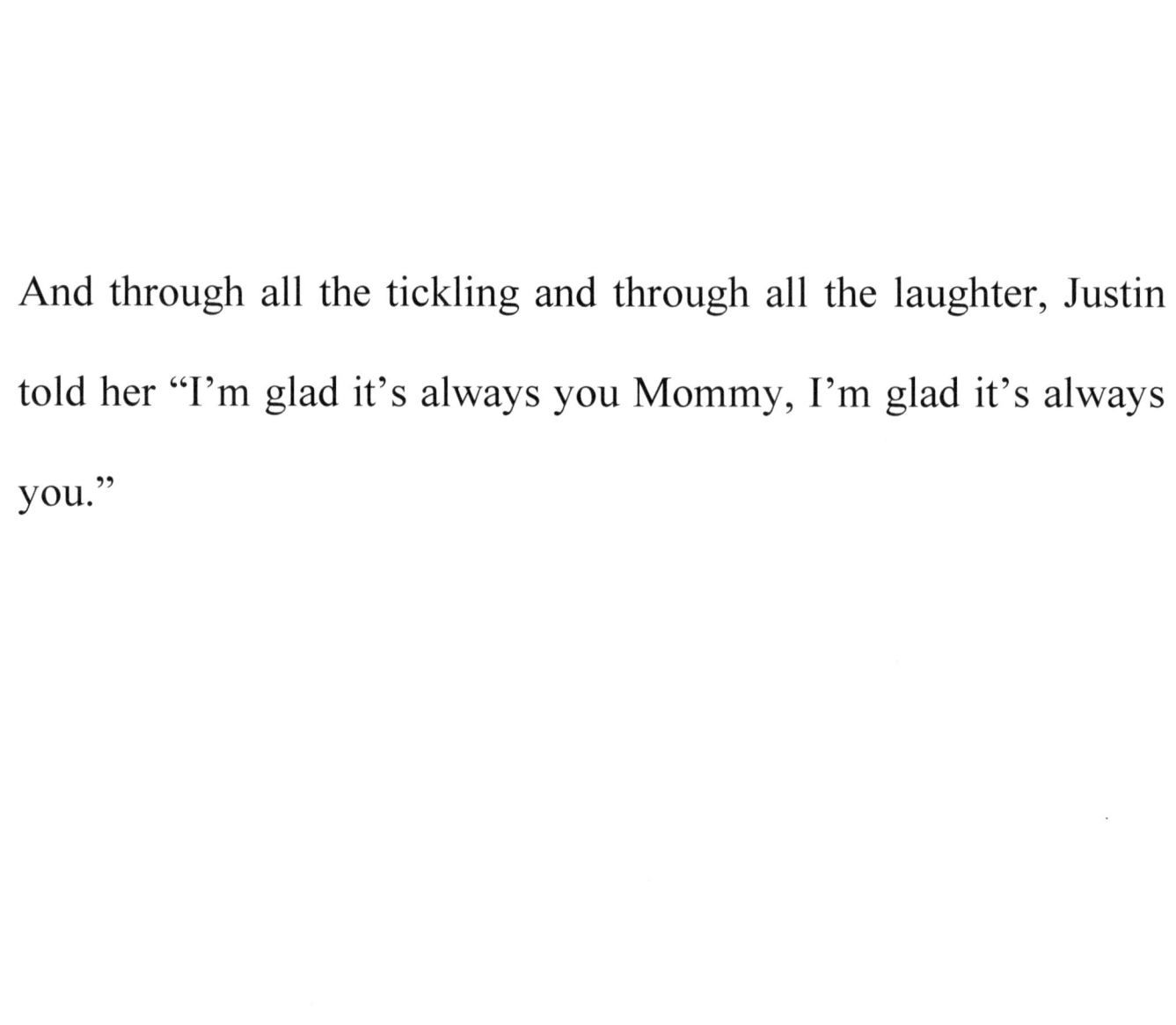

ENCOURAGING THE SINGLE MOM

"Yes You Can"

Dear Mom,

If you're reading this letter, it's because you've found yourself in the place of being a "single parent." I implore you to understand that being a single parent is in no way any fault of your own. You've decided to stand during this not so easy, tedious, yet rewarding journey. So now the next thing to do is to make a step. Put your best foot forward. Raise your child to the best of your ability, knowing this; YOU CAN DO IT. You're strong, and WITH GOD'S HELP THERE'S NOTHING YOU CAN'T DO. There's a verse of scripture from the Bible that says "I can do all things through Christ which strengthens me" (Philippians 4:13). Yet you've got to do more than just read it. You need to see it, believe it, swallow it, walk it and LIVE IT!!

Today because there is such an overwhelming demand on the single parent, things are not always as simple, easy and free-flowing, as we'd like them to be. The truth of the matter, just like anyone else, as single parents we have to deal with life too. Although it may sometimes seem like much pressure, we're not exempt. We don't get a "bypass the tough stuff" card. Yet it's all in how we handle it, which makes the difference.

Real talk. As single parents, we may have to contend with little or no support (and if you're thinking, it's not fair – YOU'RE RIGHT, IT'S NOT FAIR). There may be bills and money issues. There may be problems on the job. The other parent, if involved, may be difficult to deal with, acting unfavorably. His presence may even be like a ghost "invisible." Then to compound everything, the kids may be driving you up the wall. So what do you do?

Unfortunately, through a bout of frustration, sometimes the answer for many single parents is to take it out on the child. Now let's take a "skinny dipping moment" and be honest with ourselves. No matter what the annoyance may stem from, the job, finances, the child's father and or etc. – the child SHOULD NOT BE PENALIZED/PUNISHED BECAUSE OF OUR FRUSTRATION. Our frustration is our frustration. It shouldn't be spilled over into the child. Our children did not ask to be born. We made that decision. Children shouldn't have to shoulder "adult woes."

Oftentimes, as single moms being disappointed with the child's father, we don't allow ourselves the much-needed healing we deserve. There's shock, drama and the trauma of what we didn't expect. We didn't expect to be raising a child with "A-WOLF," "**A**bsent **W**ith**o**ut **L**eave **F**ather." Perhaps we thought... or maybe he told us he would be there.

I'm here to tell you "build a bridge, get over it, blow it up and don't look back!" Don't fully close the door either. If the Dad wants to be there for the child (since the bridge has been blown up), let him swim, float or tread water to get there to be with his child. Make no mistake about it, if he wants to, HE WILL. Your job is to trust God. Take it to Him in prayer and leave it there. It's no longer yours. So trust Him for the outcome and don't pick it up again.

If you want it, today can be a new day, a brand new start for you. It's time to walk into the total healing God has for you. Stop telling your child or children what a bad father they have. Stop sharing all the negative things about the Father and what he has or has not done for you or in the child's life. After all, the child did not choose either of you as parents. It doesn't matter that the "thrill is gone" he's still your child's father. Instead, be the nurturer, the first teacher, the loving mother and Godly example God has called you to be.

Choose to be like the woman in the Bible who (past tense) HAD, "the issue of blood." KNOW, TRUST and BELIEVE IN FAITH this day, that whatever your issue, is, if you would just REACH OUT and TOUCH THE HEM OF THE MASTER'S, (Jesus') GARMENT... **THE ISSUE WILL BE SETTLED!**

ABOUT THE AUTHOR:

Dawn Sher-Re' Barclift epitomizes integrity, hard-work and motivation. Born and bred in Newark, NJ. A singer, author and a great mom. She deeply believes that people don't have to settle for less, whether much has been made available to them or not. Dawn's attitude is "keep on pressing for the blessing." Her book, It's Always You Mommy" deals with the subject of the Absent Dad. As much as it is a children's book, it also offers tangible lessons for the single Mom.

Dawn holds an M.Div. from New York Theological Seminary. She is an ambitious, resilient, inspiring and an impactful woman. Her enthusiasm consistently spawns an unwavering drive to contribute greatly to her community and also set a Godly example for love and compassion. Additionally, she has a heart concerning the things of God and truly believes that "We are our brother's keeper." Dawn is passionate about helping every single mom come to the understanding that their lives are powerful, coupled with purpose waiting to be lived. The single mother of one currently resides in Montclair, New Jersey.

www.ingramcontent.com/pod-product-compliance
Lightning Source LLC
Chambersburg PA
CBHW040100160426
43193CB00002B/32